STORE WINDOW
SCHAUFENSTER VITRINE
ESCAPARATE VETRINA
DESIGN

teNeues

Editor: Aurora Cuito

Copy editing: Susana González

Layout: Ignasi Gracia Blanco

Translations: Alda Ferraz (French and English),
Susanne Engler (German), Maurizio Siliato (Italian)

Produced by Loft Publications
www.loftpublications.com

Published by teNeues Publishing Group

teNeues Publishing Company
16 West 22nd Street, New York, NY 10010, USA
Tel.: 001-212-627-9090, Fax: 001-212-627-9511

teNeues Book Division
Kaistraße 18
40221 Düsseldorf, Germany
Tel.: 0049-(0)211-994597-0, Fax: 0049-(0)211-994597-40

teNeues Publishing UK Ltd.
P.O. Box 402
West Byfleet
KT14 7ZF, Great Britain
Tel.: 0044-1932-403509, Fax: 0044-1932-403514

teNeues France S.A.R.L.
4, rue de Valence
75005 Paris, France
Tel.: 0033-1-55 76 62 05, Fax: 0033-1-55 76 64 19

www.teneues.com

ISBN: 3-8327-9036-5

D.L.B.: B-16718-2005

© 2005 teNeues Verlag GmbH + Co. KG, Kempen

Printed in Spain

Bibliographic information published by
Die Deutsche Bibliothek. Die Deutsche Bibliothek lists
this publication in the Deutsche Nationalbibliografie;
detailed bibliographic data is available in the Internet
at http://dnb.ddb.de.

COLOR

10-51

ILLUMINATION

52-81

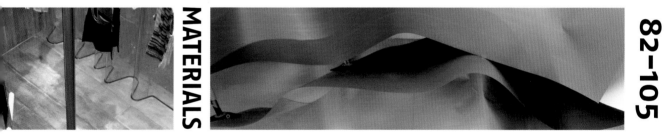

MATERIALS

82-105

FURNITURE

106-135

INTRODUCTION

EINLEITUNG

INTRODUCTION

INTRODUCCIÓN

INTRODUZIONE

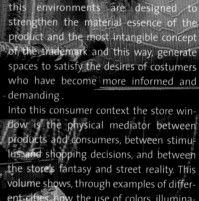

In the last decades, going shopping has become an activity so usual and common that is more related to leisure and pleasure than to the need of supply which is no longer as important as it was. Stores and shopping centres have become important scenarios and landscapes in social activity. The companies have been studying the repercussions of architecture and the design in stores for years, and they conclude by saying that they are very important factors when it comes to selling their product successfully. It is not bizarre that this environments are designed to strengthen the material essence of the product and the most intangible concept of the trademark and this way, generate spaces to satisfy the desires of costumers who have become more informed and demanding .

Into this consumer context the store window is the physical mediator between products and consumers, between stimulus and shopping decisions, and between the store's fantasy and street reality. This volume shows, through examples of different cities, how the use of colors, illumination, furniture and materials guarantee the costumer's interest on the product and the trademark's philosophy.

In den letzten Jahrzehnten ist das Einkaufen zu einer so alltäglichen Aktivität geworden, dass man es mehr mit Freizeit und Vergnügen als mit der Notwendigkeit der Versorgung, die auf die zweite Stelle gerückt ist, in Verbindung bringt. Geschäfte und Einkaufszentren sind zu wichtigen Bühnen und Landschaften von sozialen Aktivitäten geworden. Die Unternehmen analysieren schon seit Jahren die Auswirkungen der Architektur und der Innengestaltung in den Geschäften und sind zu dem Schluss gekommen, dass beide entscheidende Faktoren beim erfolgreichen Verkauf eines Produktes sind. Deshalb ist es auch nicht verwunderlich, dass das Umfeld der Produkte so gestaltet wird, dass das Wesentliche des Produktes und das weniger greifbare Konzept der Marke unterstrichen werden. So entstehen Räume, die eine immer anspruchsvollere und besser informierte Käuferschaft zufriedenstellen.

In diesem Kontext des Konsums wirkt das Schaufenster wie der physische Vermittler zwischen den Produkten und den Verbrauchern, zwischen den Reizen und der Kaufentscheidung, zwischen der Phantasie des Shops und der Wirklichkeit auf der Straße. In diesem Band wird anhand von Beispielen aus verschiedenen Städten dargestellt, wie durch den Einsatz von Farbe, Beleuchtung, Möbeln und Materialien das Interesse des Käufers für das Produkt und die Markenphilosophie geweckt wird.

Dans les dernières décennies, acheter s'est transformé en une activité si commune qu'elle est de plus en plus liée avec le loisir et le plaisir, et la besoin habituel de s'approvisionner est resté en second plan. Des magasins et des centres commerciaux sont devenues des scènes et des paysages prédominants de l'activité sociale. Les entreprises analysent depuis plusieurs années la répercussion de l'architecture et la création des magasins et concluent qu'ils sont des facteurs déterminants au moment de vendre leur produit avec succès. Il ne faut pas s'étonner que ces atmosphères sont projetées pour renforcer l'essence matérielle du produit et le concept le plus intangible de la marque, et ainsi produire des espaces pour satisfaire les désirs des acheteurs, chaque fois plus informés et exigeants.

Dans ce contexte de consommation, la vitrine s'élève comme le médiateur physique entre les produits et les consommateurs, entre stimulants et décisions d'achat, entre la fantaisie du magasin et la réalité de la rue. Ce volume expose, au moyen d'exemples dans différentes villes, comment l'utilisation de la couleur, l'éclairage, l'apport de meubles et la choix de matériaux garantissent l'intérêt de l'acheteur pour le produit et pour la philosophie de la marque.

En las últimas décadas, comprar se ha convertido en una actividad tan común que cada vez se relaciona más con el ocio y el placer, y la habitual necesidad de abastecimiento ha quedado en un segundo plano. Tiendas y centros comerciales han pasado a ser escenarios y paisajes predominantes de la actividad social. Las empresas ya llevan años analizando la repercusión de la arquitectura y el diseño de las tiendas y concluyen que son factores determinantes a la hora de vender exitosamente su producto. No es de extrañar que estos ambientes se proyecten para potenciar la esencia material del producto y el concepto más intangible de la marca, y así generar espacios para satisfacer los deseos de los compradores, cada vez más informados y exigentes.

En este contexto consumista, el escaparate se erige como el mediador físico entre productos y consumidores, entre estímulos y decisiones de compra, entre la fantasía de la tienda y la realidad de la calle. Este volumen expone, mediante ejemplos en diferentes ciudades, en qué medida la utilización del color, la iluminación, la inclusión de muebles y la selección de materiales garantizan el interés del comprador por el producto y por la filosofía de la marca.

Negli ultimi anni, fare compere è diventata un'attività così comune che si associa sempre di più allo svago e al piacere, mentre l'intrinseca necessità di approvvigionamento è passata ormai in un secondo piano. Negozi e centri commerciali si sono trasformati in scenari e paesaggi predominanti della nostra attività sociale. Dagli studi e dalle analisi svolte per conto delle aziende sulla ripercussione positiva dell'architettura e del design dei loro negozi, si deduce che questi sono fattori determinanti che aiutano a vendere con successo i propri prodotti. Non deve stupirci pertanto se questi ambienti vengano progettati con l'obiettivo di potenziare l'essenza materiale del prodotto e il concetto più intangibile della marca, generando spazi volti a soddisfare i desideri degli acquirenti, sempre più informati ed esigenti.

In questo contesto consumistico, la vetrina si pone come mediatore fisico tra i prodotti e i consumatori, tra stimoli e decisioni d'acquisto, tra la fantasia del negozio e la realtà della strada. Questo volume mostra, mediante esempi in diverse città, come l'uso del colore, l'illuminazione, l'impiego di mobili e la scelta dei materiali garantiscono l'interesse del consumatore per il prodotto e per la filosofia della marca.

Color
Die Farbe
La couleur
El color
Il colore

There is a great variety of scientific research that, after analysing the physical status of colors, conclude by saying that the chromatic phenomenon is the result of the decomposition of white light to create a wide range of colors. In spite of the theory of colors being so complex and rich, its sensitive and perceptive conditions are those to be studied by a storage window designer. Colors produce an immediate stimulus that really lasts and brings with it a lot of information for the observer and for the potential client. Using colors is one of the easiest and more economical techniques to transform spaces, and make them become larger or more compact, colder or warmer or more eye-catching or fine.

The psychological reactions that colors provoke are very effective and varied: white makes spaces bigger and allows a better perception of the goods displayed in the windows, black ends with the volumetric sense of the window and needs a certain light, red usually steps off the facade and floods the outside. Besides the contrasted combinations of colors, variations of a certain shade may also be used because they allow generating a rich deepness and give the area of display a defined nature. This rules of colors' language must be taken just as a reference, there are not right or wrong combinations of colors but we must look for coherence with the objects displayed and, of course, for harmony with the rest of elements.

Es gibt eine ganze Reihe von wissenschaftlichen Untersuchungen, die die physischen Bedingungen der Farbe analysieren und zu dem Schluss kommen, dass das Phänomen Farbe ein Produkt der Zerlegung des weißen Lichts in ein weites Farbspektrum ist. Die Farbtheorie ist sehr komplex und umfassend, aber was für den Schaufenstergestalter besonders wichtig ist, sind die Empfindungen und Wahrnehmungen, die durch Farben hervorgerufen werden. Farben stellen einen unmittelbaren und dauerhaften Reiz mit einem großen Inhalt an Informationen für den Beobachter und potentiellen Kunden dar. Die Verwendung von Farben ist eine der einfachsten und preisgünstigsten Techniken, einen Raum zu gestalten, ihn weiter oder enger, kalt oder warm, grell oder subtil wirken zu lassen.

Farben rufen echte und verschiedenartige, psychologische Reaktionen hervor: Weiß lässt Räume größer wirken und die ausgestellten Waren sind gut sichtbar, durch Schwarz verliert das Schaufenster an räumlicher Wirkung und man benötigt eine bestimmte Beleuchtung. Rot scheint sich nach draußen auszudehnen. Außer miteinander kontrastierender Farben werden oft Variationen eines gleichen Farbtons benutzt, durch die eine weite Skala von Tiefen entsteht und die dem Ausstellungsbereich einen klar definierten Charakter verleihen. Die Regeln dafür, wie Farben zu benutzen sind, dienen nur als Anhaltspunkt. Es gibt keine richtigen oder falschen Kombinationen, sondern es müssen der Zusammenhang zwischen den ausgestellten Objekten und die Harmonie mit den anderen Dekorationselementen hergestellt werden.

Il existe une grande variété d'études scientifiques qui, après avoir analysé les conditions physiques de la couleur, concluent que le phénomène chromatique est le produit de la décomposition de la lumière blanche pour former un vaste spectre de couleurs. Malgré la complexité et la richesse de la théorie de la couleur, ce sont ses conditions sensibles et perceptives qui doivent faire l'objet d'une étude par un décorateur de vitrines. Les couleurs produisent un stimulant immédiat, durable et d'un grand contenu informatif pour l'observateur et le client potentiel. L'application de la couleur est une des techniques les plus simples et économiques pour transformer l'espace, afin de rendre l'atmosphère plus vaste ou compacte, froide ou chaude, frappante ou subtile.

Les réactions psychologiques produites par les couleurs sont effectives et variées : le blanc agrandit les espaces et permet une meilleure perception des marchandises exposées, le noir élimine la sensation de volume de la vitrine et oblige à une illumination déterminée, le rouge tend à sortir de la façade et inonder l'extérieur. Outre les combinaisons chromatiques contrastées, on utilise aussi fréquemment les variations sur un même ton, puisqu'elles permettent de produire une riche échelle de profondeurs et accordent un caractère défini au secteur d'exposition. Les règles du langage de la couleur doivent être seulement considérées comme une référence, il n'existe pas de combinaisons correctes ou incorrectes, mais on doit évidemment chercher la cohérence avec les objets exposés et l'harmonie avec les outres éléments.

Existe una gran variedad de estudios científicos que, tras analizar las condiciones físicas del color, concluyen que el fenómeno cromático es el producto de la descomposición de la luz blanca para formar un amplio espectro de colores. A pesar de la complejidad y la riqueza de la teoría del color, son sus condiciones sensibles y perceptivas las que deben ser objeto de estudio por parte de un diseñador de escaparates. Los colores producen un estímulo inmediato, perdurable y de gran contenido informativo para el observador y cliente potencial. La aplicación del color es una de las técnicas más sencillas y económicas para transformar el espacio, convertirlo en un ambiente más amplio o compacto, frío o cálido, llamativo o sutil.

Las reacciones psicológicas producidas por los colores son efectivas y variadas: el blanco agranda los espacios y permite una mejor percepción de las mercancías expuestas, el negro elimina la sensación volumétrica del escaparate y obliga a una iluminación determinada, el rojo tiende a salirse de la fachada e inundar el exterior. Además de las combinaciones cromáticas contrastadas, también se utilizan frecuentemente las variaciones de un mismo tono, ya que permiten generar una rica escala de profundidades y otorgan un carácter definido al área de exposición. Las reglas del lenguaje del color deben ser tomadas sólo como una referencia, no existen combinaciones correctas o incorrectas, sino que debe buscarse la coherencia con los objetos expuestos y evidentemente la armonía con los demás elementos.

Esiste un gran numero di studi scientifici che, dopo aver analizzato le condizioni fisiche del colore, concludono affermando che il fenomeno cromatico è il prodotto della decomposizione della luce bianca per formare un ampio spettro di colori. Nonostante la teoria del colore sia un tema complesso e denso, un disegnatore di vetrine deve almeno essere a conoscenza delle percezioni e le sensazioni suscitate dai colori. Questi producono uno stimolo immediato, durevole e di gran contenuto informativo per l'osservatore e potenziale cliente. L'applicazione del colore è una delle tecniche più semplici ed economiche per trasformare lo spazio, convertirlo in un ambiente più ampio o compatto, freddo o accogliente, appariscente o sobrio.

Le reazioni psicologiche prodotte dai colori sono efficaci e di vario tipo: il bianco ingrandisce gli spazi e consente una migliore percezione dei prodotti esposti, il nero elimina la sensazione volumetrica della vetrina ed obbliga a un determinato tipo di illuminazione, il rosso tende a oltrepassare i limiti fisici della vetrina e inondare l'esterno. Oltre ai già consolidati accostamenti cromatici, frequentemente si usano pure le variazioni di uno stesso tono, in quanto permettono di generare una ricca scala di profondità e conferiscono un carattere più definito all'area di esposizione. Le regole del linguaggio dei colori vanno prese soltanto come un riferimento, non esistono abbinamenti giusti o sbagliati; si deve, invece, cercare la coerenza con gli oggetti esposti ed evidentemente l'armonia con gli altri elementi.

Gonzalo Comella

Photography: Louis Bou Romero
Barcelona, Spain

Gonzalo Comella

The drawer Jordi Labanda was responsible for drawing some characters on the window's background and also on the facades glass. They were combined with real manikins, complements and clothes.

Der Illustrator Jordi Labanda zeichnete einige Figuren auf den Hintergrund des Schaufensters und auf das Schaufensterglas. Diese wurden mit echten Schaufensterpuppen, Accessoires und Kleidungsstücken kombiniert.

L'illustrateur Jordi Labanda fut les responsable de dessiner plusieurs personnages sur le fond de la vitrine et aussi sur le vitre de la façade. Ils ont été combinés avec des mannequins, compléments et vêtements réels.

El ilustrador Jordi Labanda fue el responsable de dibujar varios personajes sobre el fondo del escaparate y también sobre el cristal de la fachada. Se combinaron con maniquíes, complementos y piezas de ropa reales.

All'illustratore Jordi Labanda è stato affidato il compito di disegnare vari personaggi sullo sfondo della vetrina e pure sulla vetrata della facciata. Il tutto viene completato da manichini, accessori e capi da abbigliamento reali.

Louis Vuitton

Photography: David Cardelús   Design: Peter Marino & Associates
Paris, France

Christian Lacroix

Photography: Nacása & Partners Inc.   Design: Caps Architects
Tokyo, Japan

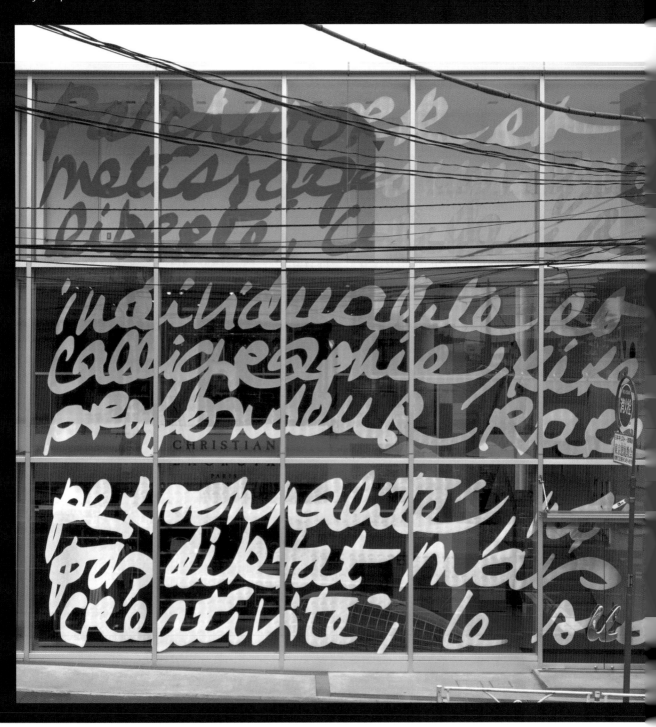

The use of colors in this store is obvious in various parts of the design, from graphic multicolored application of the glass facade to the display stands of dyed methachrylate.

Farbe spielt in der Gestaltung dieser Räume eine wichtige Rolle, angefangen bei der bunten Grafik auf der Glasfassade bis hin zu den Ausstellungsmöbeln aus gefärbtem Metacrylat.

L'utilisation de la couleur dans ce local est évidente dans plusieurs aspects de la création, depuis l'application graphique multicolore de la façade de cristal jusqu'aux meubles expositoires de méthacrylate teint.

La utilización del color en este local se hace evidente en varios aspectos del diseño, desde la aplicación gráfica multicolor de la fachada de cristal hasta los muebles expositores de metacrilato tintado.

L'uso del colore in questo locale si manifesta in vari aspetti del design, dall'applicazione grafica multicolore della facciata di vetro fino ai mobili espositori di metacrilato colorato.

Bershka

Photography: Louis Bou Romero
Barcelona, Spain

1960's pop art is an appealing tendency either by its effectiveness in composition or by its flashy colors, and Bershka reinvents it to present their summer collection.

Die Pop-Art der Sechzigerjahre ist aufgrund der Wirkung ihrer Kompositionen als auch der auffallenden Farben ein immer wiederkehrender Trend. Die Firma Bershka interpretiert diesen Stil neu, um ihre Sommerkollektion vorzustellen.

Le pop art des années 1960 est une tendance récurrente soit par son efficacité de composition soit par les couleurs voyantes, et Bershka le réinvente pour présenter sa collection d'été.

El pop art de los años sesenta es una tendencia recurrente, ya sea por su efectividad compositiva ya por sus colores llamativos, y Bershka lo reinventa para presentar su colección de verano.

La Pop Art degli anni 60' è un motivo decorativo ricorrente, sia per la sua efficacia compositiva che per i suoi sgargianti colori, e Bershka lo rivisita per presentare la sua collezione estiva.

Prada

Photography: Louis Bou Romero
London, United Kingdom

Prada has used very eye-catching shining panels to catch the attention of passers. When the observer gets closer to it, he can perceive a refined design tables where a few of this trademark products are placed.

Prada hat einige sehr auffallende, glänzende Paneele benutzt, um die Aufmerksamkeit der Passanten auf sich zu ziehen. Wenn der Betrachter sich nähert, sieht er Tische in edlem Design, auf denen sich verschiedene Produkte der Firma befinden.

Prada a utilisé des panneaux brillants très voyants pour attirer l'attention des passants. Quand l'observateur s'approche, il peut apercevoir des tables de création raffinée sur lesquelles sont placés plusieurs produits de la marque.

Prada ha utilizado unos paneles brillantes muy llamativos para captar la atención de los transeúntes. Cuando el observador se acerca, puede percibir unas mesas de diseño refinado donde se colocan varios productos de la firma.

Prada ha utilizzato dei pannelli brillanti molto appariscenti per attirare l'attenzione dei passanti. Avvicinandosi alla vetrina, l'osservatore può percepire dei tavoli dal design raffinato su cui sono disposti vari prodotti della griffe.

Dickins & Jones

Photography: Louis Bou Romero
London, United Kingdom

Yourself

fashion to make your heart flutter

Jump for joy

Leap

A little animal decoration, as butterflies or bees, are enough to liven up this store's windows which are totally painted with flashy colors in harmony with the manikin's garments.

Kleine Tiermotive wie Schmetterlinge oder Bienen genügen, um die Schaufenster dieses Shops zu beleben. Sie sind passend zu den Kleidungsstücken der Schaufensterpuppen in auffallenden Farben gehalten.

Un petit motif animal, comme des papillons ou des abeilles, suffisent pour animer les vitrines de cette boutique, entièrement peintes de couleurs vives en harmonie avec les vêtements des mannequins.

Un pequeño motivo animal, como son unas mariposas o unas abejas, bastan para amenizar los escaparates de esta tienda, pintados enteramente de colores llamativos en armonía con las prendas de los maniquíes.

Un piccolo motivo animale, come possono essere delle coccinelle o delle api, basta per vivacizzare le vetrine di questo negozio, dipinte interamente in colori vistosi, abbinati ai capi indossati dai manichini.

Bee Yourself

fashion that creates a buzz

Burberry

Photography: Louis Bou Romero
Barcelona, Spain

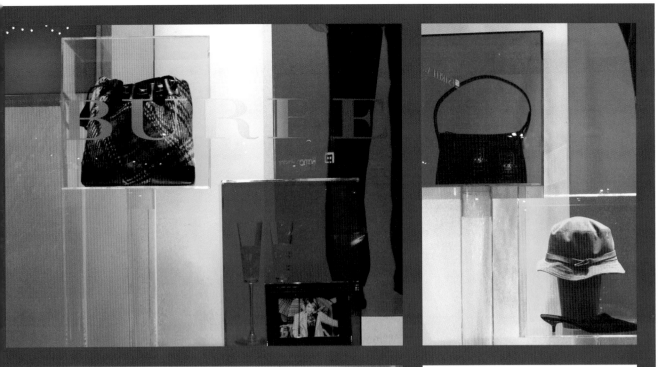

Colors are imposed over the clothes in this Burberry's store window, where garments are placed in colored methachrylate cubicles. In some cases, this material's transparency allows various colors to unite themselves in one new color.

Die Farbe wird in diesem Schaufenster der Firma Burberry über die Kleidung gelegt, indem die Kleidungsstücke in Kammern aus buntem Metacrylat präsentiert werden. In einigen Fällen lässt die Transparenz dieses Materials mehrere Farben zu einer neuen verschmelzen.

La couleur s'impose aux vêtements dans cette vitrine de Burberry, où les articles ont été placés dans les étagères de méthacrylate de couleurs. Dans certains cas, la transparence de ce matériel fait que plusieurs couleurs se fondent en une seule.

El color se impone a la ropa en este escaparate de la firma Burberry, donde las prendas se colocaron en cubículos de metacrilato de colores. En algunos casos, la transparencia de este material permite que varios colores se fundan en uno nuevo.

Il colore prevale sulle merci esposte in questa vetrina della maison Burberry, dove i capi sono stati disposti dentro cubicoli di metacrilato colorato. In alcuni casi, la trasparenza di questo materiale fa sì che vari colori si fondano in uno nuovo.

Illumination
Die Beleuchtung
L'éclairage
La iluminación
L'illuminazione

Aesthetic values of light are endless and the ability of transforming spaces and give them their own personality make light become one the most powerful tools in windows designing. When referring to a system of seduction so complex as lighting, we need to distinguish within three areas of analysis: the project's conceptual aim, the constructive techniques and tools we have to carry it out and the aesthetic result of the staging of the window. We also have to take into account the natural and artificial light impact, bearing in mind that the first one has fixed cycles and the second one can be manipulated depending on commercial needs. The lighting of a window does not consist in just giving light to a certain space but it also stresses the products and creates a specific environment. The type of product and the wished effect to frame it are the premises that the designers take as starting point. Besides, the illuminance (quantity of light that a surface receives), brightness (quantity of light that gets from the surface), color temperature (apparent color of light) and the chromatic reproduction rate (the ability of a source of light to reproduce faithfully the colors that illuminates) are also important. Studying these factors will allow us to choose correctly the instruments, and accomplish a design of a flexible system regarding movement and qualities of light in order to be able to adapt to the constant changes that take place in the distribution of stores.

Licht ist ein sehr wichtiges ästhetisches Element. Es kann Räume umformen und ihnen eine eigene Persönlichkeit verleihen, was es zu einem der wichtigsten Instrumente für die Schaufenstergestaltung macht. Für die Beschreibung eines so komplexen Instruments der Verführung wie der Beleuchtung muss man drei Analysebereiche unterscheiden, das Ziel des Projektkonzeptes, die konstruktiven Techniken und Mittel, um dieses umzusetzen, und das ästhetische Ergebnis, das durch die Umsetzung im Schaufenster erreicht wird. Außerdem muss auf den unterschiedlichen Einfall von Tageslicht und künstlichem Licht geachtet werden. Tageslicht ist von festen Zeiten abhängig, während künstliches Licht je nach den kommerziellen Bedürfnissen eingesetzt werden kann. Wenn man ein Schaufenster beleuchtet, beleuchtet man nicht nur einen bestimmten Raum, sondern man hebt auch Produkte hervor und schafft eine bestimmte Atmosphäre. Die Art des Produktes und die gewünschte Wirkung sind die Voraussetzungen, die dem Schaufenstergestalter als Ausgangspunkt dienen. Außerdem sind die Faktoren Beleuchtungsstärke (die von einer Oberfläche erhaltene Lichtmenge), Leuchtdichte (Lichtmenge, die zu einer Oberfläche gelangt), Farbtemperatur (die sichtbare Farbe des Lichtes) und der Farbwiedergabeindex (die Kapazität einer Lichtquelle, genau die Farben, die es beleuchtet, wiederzugeben) von Bedeutung. Nur unter Berücksichtigung all dieser Faktoren ist eine korrekte Auswahl der notwendigen Instrumente möglich. Ziel ist ein flexibles System für die Bewegungen und Eigenschaften des Lichtes, das sich an die sich ständig verändernde Raumeinteilung eines Geschäftes anpassen kann.

Les valeurs esthétiques de la lumière sont infinies et la capacité de transformer des espaces et de les doter de leur propre personnalité font qu'elle représente un des instruments les plus importants dans la création de vitrines. En se référant à un système de séduction aussi complexe que l'éclairage il est nécessaire de distinguer trois secteurs d'analyse : l'objectif conceptuel du projet, les techniques et les moyens constructifs pour le mener à bien, et le résultat esthétique qui est obtenu avec la mise en scène de la vitrine. Il faut aussi prendre en considération la différente incidence de l'éclairage naturelle et l'artificiel, puisque le premier a des cycles fixes et le deuxième peut être manipulé en fonction des demandes commerciales. L'éclairage d'une vitrine ne consiste pas seulement à éclairer un espace déterminé, mais elle a aussi la mission de mettre en valeur les produits et de créer une certaine ambiance. Le genre de produit et l'effet souhaité pour les encadrer sont les prémices que les dessinateurs prennent comme point de départ. De plus, entrent aussi en jeu l'éclairement (quantité de lumière que reçoit une unité de surface), la luminance (quotient de l'intensité lumineuse émise par une surface) la température de la couleur (la couleur apparente de la lumière), et l'indice de reproduction chromatique (la capacité d'une source de lumière de reproduire fidèlement les couleurs qu'elle illumine). L'étude de ces facteurs permettra un bon choix des instruments qui aboutira à la création d'un système flexible quant à mouvement et qualités de la lumière, afin de s'adapter aux changements constants qui se succèdent dans la distribution d'un magasin.

Los valores estéticos de la luz son infinitos y la capacidad de transformar espacios y dotarlos de personalidad propia la convierten en uno de los instrumentos más potentes en el diseño de escaparates. Al referirnos a un sistema de seducción tan complejo como la iluminación es necesario distinguir tres áreas de análisis: el objetivo conceptual del proyecto, las técnicas y medios constructivos para llevarlo a cabo, y el resultado estético que se consigue en la puesta a escena del escaparate. También se debe tener en cuenta la distinta incidencia de la iluminación natural y la de la artificial, ya que la primera tiene unos ciclos fijos y la segunda puede manipularse en función de los requerimientos comerciales. La iluminación de un escaparate no consiste sólo en alumbrar un espacio determinado, sino que también se encarga de destacar los productos y de crear un ambiente específico. El tipo de producto y el efecto deseado para enmarcarlo son las premisas que los diseñadores toman como punto de partida. Además, también entran en juego la iluminancia (cantidad de luz recibida por una superficie), la luminancia (cantidad de luz que llega de la superficie), la temperatura del color (el color aparente de la luz) y el índice de reproducción cromática (la capacidad de una fuente de luz de reproducir fielmente los colores que alumbra). El estudio de estos factores permitirá una acertada elección de los instrumentos que culminará con el diseño de un sistema flexible en cuanto a movimiento y calidades de luz, para poder adaptarse a los constantes cambios que se suceden en la distribución de una tienda.

I valori estetici della luce sono infiniti. La capacità di trasformare spazi e dotarli di una propria personalità fa della luce uno degli strumenti più potenti per ciò che riguarda il disegno e l'allestimento di vetrine. Riferendosi a un sistema di seduzione così complesso come l'illuminazione, è necessario distinguere tre aree di analisi: l'obiettivo concettuale del progetto, le tecniche e i mezzi costruttivi per portarlo a termine, e il risultato estetico che si ottiene una volta addobbata la vetrina. Un altro fattore da tenere in considerazione è la diversa incidenza dell'illuminazione naturale e di quella artificiale, visto che la prima presenta dei cicli fissi mentre la seconda può modificarsi a seconda delle specifiche esigenze commerciali. L'illuminazione di una vetrina non consiste soltanto nell'illuminare uno determinato spazio, ma ha anche la funzione di mettere in risalto i prodotti e creare un particolare ambiente. Nel momento di allestire uno spazio espositivo, i vetrinisti prendono come punto di partenza il tipo di prodotto e l'effetto che desiderano produrre. Inoltre, entrano in gioco anche altri fattori quali l'illuminamento (quantità di luce che riceve una superficie), la luminanza (quantità di luce che proviene dalla superficie), la temperatura del colore (il colore apparente della luce) e l'indice di riproduzione cromatica (la capacità di una fonte di luce di riprodurre fedelmente i colori che illumina). Lo studio di questi fattori consentirà di scegliere bene gli strumenti e di realizzare un sistema flessibile in quanto a movimento e qualità di luce, in grado di adattarsi ai costanti cambiamenti che si verificano nella distribuzione del negozio.

M-Premier

Photography: Fumita Design Office
Tokyo, Japan

This project itself is a great lighting system, where each of its elements has light functions, as the steel and glass boxes from which the garments are hanging or the floodlight's trenches on the ceiling.

Dieses Projekt ist eigentlich ein großes Beleuchtungssystem, in dem jedes Element Leuchtfunktionen erfüllt, wie zum Beispiel die großen Kisten aus Stahl und Glas, von denen Kleidungsstücke oder die Scheinwerferleisten der Decke hängen.

Ce projet est en lui-même un grand système d'éclairage, où chacun de ses éléments a des fonctions lumineuses, comme les grandes caisses d'acier et cristal d'où pendent les vêtements ou bien les projecteurs incorporés dans le plafond.

Este proyecto es en sí mismo un gran sistema de iluminación, donde cada uno de sus elementos tiene funciones lumínicas, como las grandes cajas de acero y cristal desde donde cuelgan las prendas o las zanjas de focos en el techo.

Di per sé, questo progetto è un grande sistema di illuminazione, dove ognuno dei suoi elementi possiede una determinata funzione luminosa, come le grandi casse di acciaio e vetro da dove pendono gli abiti o gli incassi dei faretti nel soffitto.

Malo

Photography: Matteo Piazza   Design: Claudio Nardi
Milan, Italy

Light tonalities for the walls and dark specific objects constitute the aesthetic lines of this store's windows, where the garments are main protagonists.

Helle Töne für die Wandverkleidung und einzelne, dunkle Objekte prägen die ästhetische Linie der Schaufenster dieses Shops, in dem die Kleidungsstücke die unbestrittenen Hauptdarsteller sind.

Tonalités claires pour le murs et objets obscurs ponctuels constituent les lignes esthétiques des vitrines de ce magasin, où les articles sont des protagonistes indiscutables.

Tonalidades claras para las paredes y objetos oscuros que la salpican constituyen las líneas estéticas de los escaparates de esta tienda, donde las prendas son protagonistas indiscutibles.

Tonalità chiare per le pareti e specifici oggetti scuri costituiscono le linee estetiche delle vetrine di questo negozio dove i capi di abbigliamento sono gli indiscussi protagonisti.

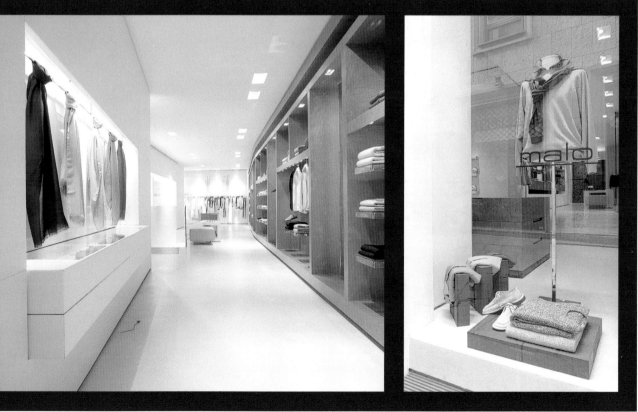

Costume National

Photography: Benny Chan

Los Angeles, USA

The hangers are fixed to parameters which stick out of the vertical divisions of the store and which add a diffuse lighting system that is complemented with the one from the direct floodlights built in the ceiling.

Die Kleiderbügel sind an Wandflächen befestigt, die aus den vertikalen Raumteilern des Shops hervorstehen und mit einem diffusen Beleuchtungssystem ausgestattet sind, das durch die direkten Scheinwerfer, die in der Decke eingebaut sind, ergänzt wird.

Les cintres sont fixés à des ornements qui sortent des divisions verticales du magasin et contiennent un système d'éclairage diffus qui se complémente avec celui des projecteurs directs encastrés dans le plafond.

Los colgadores están fijados a unos paramentos que sobresalen de las particiones verticales de la tienda y que incorporan un sistema de iluminación difusa que se complementa con la de los focos directos empotrados en el techo.

Gli appendiabiti sono fissati a dei paramenti che sporgono dalle divisioni verticali del negozio; a questi è incorporato un sistema di illuminazione diffusa che viene completato dalla luce diretta dei faretti incassati nel soffitto.

Antonio Pernas

Photography: Eugeni Pons   Design: Iago Seara
Barcelona, Spain

Lamps hanging from the ceiling, specific lighting of architectural elements and floodlights placed strategically generate an environment in harmony with the trademark philosophy.

Durch die Lampen an der Decke, die spezielle Beleuchtung der architektonischen Elemente und die strategische Aufstellung von Scheinwerfern entsteht eine Atmosphäre, die der Markenphilosophie entspricht.

La suspension de lampes au plafond, l'éclairage spécifique d'éléments architectoniques et la mise en place stratégique de projecteurs produisent une atmosphère en accord avec la philosophie de la marque.

La suspensión de lámparas del techo, la iluminación específica de elementos arquitectónicos y la colocación estratégica de focos generan un ambiente acorde con la filosofía de la marca.

La sospensione di lampade dal soffitto, l'illuminazione specifica di elementi architettonici e la collocazione strategica di faretti generano un ambiente conforme alla filosofia della marca.

Krizia

Photography: Louis Bou Romero
Barcelona, Spain

Lighting not just is very meaningful in this store window but, it is also the store's sign: a plaster plaque with illuminated letters from the back thanks to a uniform system of lighting fittings.

Die Beleuchtung spielt nicht nur eine wichtige Rolle in diesem Schaufenster, sondern sie bildet auch das Schild dieses Shops, eine Gipsplatte mit einem einheitlichen Beleuchtungssystem, das die Buchstaben von hinten beleuchtet.

L'éclairage non seulement joue un rôle important dans la vitrine mais en outre il forme l'affiche de la boutique : une plaque de plâtre découpée avec des lettres illuminées pour derrière grâce à un système uniforme de luminaires.

La iluminación no sólo desempeña un papel significativo en el escaparate, sino que además conforma el cartel de la tienda: una placa de yeso recortada con letras iluminadas por detrás gracias a un sistema uniforme de iluminación.

L'illuminazione non solo riveste un ruolo determinante nella vetrina ma inoltre configura l'insegna del negozio: una lastra ritagliata in gesso con lettere illuminate da dietro grazie a un sistema uniforme di luci.

Materials

Die Materialien

Les matériaux

Los materiales

I materiali

The materials of the components of a store window and of the goods displayed are hard to be perceived by a distant observer, so the ability to use them will have to bear in mind the maximum approximation of the customer to the window. The texture, taken as the superficial quality of materials, defines the psychology of the area of display: using it will combine visual and tactile experiences. This fact makes the products displayed become wished objects and provokes in the observers feelings bounding them to wish the purchasing of the products.

Most materials have implicit a special sensuality that gives them their own emotional charge: The elegance and softness of silk, the warmness of wood and the lightness of glass are well-known. This language of materials and its textures must give support to the windows' conceptualisation and setting through their contrast and richness.

Sensorial effects of the materials do not just vary with the different combinations, but also depending on the season of the year and the cultural contexts where they are. Then, the metallic and glass items strengthen cold in winter while velvet and carpets compensate it. The right choices, the coherence and the seduction are all found in the harmony and in the contrast.

Die Materialien der Komponenten eines Schaufensters und die in ihm ausgestellten Waren können von weitem nicht gut wahrgenommen werden. Deshalb sollte beim Umgang mit diesen Elementen berücksichtigt werden, wie weit der Käufer an das Schaufenster herantreten kann. Die Textur, die Oberflächenqualität der Materialien, definiert das psychologische Konzept des Ausstellungsraums, sie kombiniert die visuellen mit den haptischen Erfahrungen. So werden aus den gezeigten Produkten Wunschobjekte, beim Betrachter werden Kaufwünsche erweckt.

Die meisten Materialien besitzen eine besondere Sinnlichkeit, die ihnen eine eigene, emotionsgeladene Bedeutung überträgt. Seide wirkt elegant und weich, Holz warm und Glas und Kristall sehr leicht. Diese eigene Sprache der Materialien und ihrer Texturen muss dazu benutzt werden, Schaufenster durch Kontraste und die verschiedenen Eigenschaften der Materialien in Szene zu setzen und zu betonen.

Die Wirkung, die die Materialien auf die Sinne haben, variiert nicht nur durch die möglichen Kombinationen, sondern auch durch den Lauf der Jahreszeiten und durch das unterschiedliche kulturelle Umfeld, aus dem das Material stammt. So verstärken Elemente aus Metall und Glas den Eindruck von Winterkälte, während Samt und Teppiche als Ausgleich wirken. Eine gelungene Auswahl, Geschlossenheit und Verführung können sowohl im Zusammenspiel als auch im Gegensatz zu finden sein.

Les matériaux des composants d'une vitrine, et ceux de marchandises exposées dans celle-ci, sont difficilement perceptibles par un observateur lointain, c'est pourquoi l'habilité dans l'utilisation devra tenir compte du rapprochement maximum de l'acheteur à la vitrine. La texture, une comme la qualité superficielle des matériaux, définira la psychologie de l'espace d'exposition : par leur emploi on combinera les expériences visuelles et tactiles. Ce fait convertit les produits présentés en objets souhaités et provoque dans l'observateur des sensations destinées à désirer son acquisition.

Dans la plupart des matériaux il y a une particulière sensualité implicite qui leur confère une charge émotive propre : l'élégance et la douceur de la soie est bien connue, la chaleur du bois et la légèreté du cristal. Ce langage propre des matériaux et ses textures doit soutenir la contextualisation et l'ambiance des vitrines par le contraste et la richesse de ses caractéristiques.

Les effets sensoriels des matériaux changent non seulement avec les possibles combinaisons, mais aussi selon les saisons de l'année et des évènements culturels durant lesquels ils sont situés. Ainsi, les éléments métalliques et de cristal renforcent la sensation de froid en hiver, alors que les velours et les tapis la compensent. La bonne sélection, la cohérence et la séduction se trouvent en part égale aussi bien dans l'harmonie comme dans le contraste.

Los materiales de los componentes de un escaparate, y de las mercancías expuestas en él, son difícilmente perceptibles por un observador lejano, por lo que la habilidad en la utilización deberá tener en cuenta la máxima aproximación del comprador a la vitrina. La textura, entendida como la calidad superficial de los materiales, definirá la psicología del espacio de exhibición: mediante su empleo se combinarán las experiencias visuales con las táctiles. Este hecho convierte los productos presentados en objetos deseados y provoca en el observador sensaciones destinadas a desear su adquisición.

En la mayoría de los materiales hay implícita una sensualidad particular que les confiere una carga emotiva propia: es bien conocida la elegancia y la suavidad de la seda, la calidez de la madera y la ligereza del cristal. Este lenguaje propio de los materiales y sus texturas debe apoyar la contextualización y ambientación de los escaparates mediante el contraste y la riqueza de sus características.

Los efectos sensoriales de los materiales no sólo varían con las posibles combinaciones, sino también según las estaciones del año y los contextos culturales en los que se encuentren. Así, los elementos metálicos y de cristal potencian la sensación de frío en invierno, mientras que el terciopelo y las alfombras la compensan. La selección acertada, la coherencia y la seducción se encuentran por igual tanto en la armonía como en el contraste.

I materiali dei componenti di una vetrina e delle merci in essa esposte, sono difficilmente percepibili da un osservatore che la guarda da lontano. Pertanto, l'abilità nell'uso dei materiali dovrà tenere conto del massimo avvicinamento del potenziale acquirente alla vetrina. La texture, intesa come la qualità superficiale dei materiali, definirà la psicologia dello spazio espositivo: mediante il suo utilizzo, si combineranno le esperienze visuali con quelle tattili. Ciò trasforma i prodotti presentati in oggetti desiderati e provoca in chi li osserva sensazioni che inducono a desiderare la loro acquisizione.

Nella maggior parte dei materiali vi è implicita una sensualità particolare che gli conferisce una propria carica emotiva: è ben nota l'eleganza e la morbidezza della seta, il calore del legno e la leggerezza del cristallo. Questo linguaggio tipico dei materiali e delle loro consistenze deve fare da spalla alla contestualizzazione e ambientazione delle vetrine mediante il contrasto e la ricchezza delle loro caratteristiche.

Gli effetti sensoriali dei materiali non solo cambiano con i possibili accostamenti, ma anche a secondo delle stagioni dell'anno e dei contesti culturali in cui si trovano. In questo modo, gli elementi metallici e di cristallo potenziano la sensazione di freddo in inverno, mentre il velluto e i tappeti la compensano. Sia un accostamento armonico che di contrasto possono costituire una scelta azzeccata o suscitare coerenza e seduzione.

Issey Miyake

Photography: Roger Casas   Design: Gordon Kipping
New York, USA

Issey Miyake's work is innovative and experimental and we can see these features stressed in all its stores around the world. The store in New York plays with a system of steel folds that hide an original structure of wood.

Die Kreationen von Issey Miyake sind innovativ und experimentell, was in der Gestaltung der Shops der Marke auf der ganzen Welt noch unterstrichen wird. In New York wird mit einem System von gefaltetem Stahl gespielt, das die Originalstruktur aus Holz verbirgt.

L'œuvre d'Issey Miyake est innovatrice et expérimentale, et ces caractéristiques sont soulignées dans les boutiques distribuées partout dans le monde. Dans celle de New York, il joue avec un système de plis d'acier qui cachent une originale structure de bois.

La obra de Issey Miyake es innovadora y experimental, y tales características se ven enfatizadas en las tiendas que tiene repartidas en todo el mundo. En la de Nueva York, juega con un sistema de pliegues de acero que esconden una estructura original de madera.

L'opera di Issey Miyake è innovativa e sperimentale, e tali caratteristiche vengono enfatizzate nei suoi negozi e showroom sparsi in tutto il mondo. Nel negozio di New York, gioca con un sistema di pieghe di acciaio che nascondono una struttura originale in legno.

Hare

Photography: Kozo Takayama
Tokyo, Japan

This clothes store combines recycled wood for the floor and the ceiling, white painted plaster for walls and a steel and glass furniture where the garments are displayed.

In diesem Kleidergeschäft werden Recyclingholz für die Böden und Decken, weißbemalter Gips für die Wände und Möbel aus Stahl und Glas, auf denen die Kleidungsstücke ausgestellt werden, miteinander kombiniert.

Ce magasin de vêtements combine du bois récupéré pour sol et plafonds, plâtre peint de blanc pour les murs et des meubles d'acier et cristal où l'on expose les vêtements.

Esta tienda de ropa combina madera recuperada para suelo y techos, yeso pintado de blanco para paredes y unos muebles de acero y cristal donde se exponen las prendas.

Questo negozio di abbigliamento combina legno recuperato per il pavimento e il soffitto, gesso dipinto di bianco per le pareti e alcuni mobili in acciaio e vetro dove vengono esposti gli abiti.

Tehen

Photography: Michael Moran   Design: Daniel Goldner Architects
New York, USA

Custo Barcelona

Photography: Kozo Takayama

Tokyo, Japan

This Barcelona's sign patterns, fabrics and illustrations intensity do not reduce the design of the stores which unite a great variety of materials to strengthen their image of trademark.

Die Intensität der Schnitte, Stoffe und Illustrationen dieser barcelonesischen Firma wird auch in der Gestaltung ihrer Shops fortgesetzt, die mit einer Vielzahl von Materialien dekoriert sind, die das Markenimage unterstreichen.

L'intensité des patrons, les tissus et les illustrations de la marque barcelonaise ne diminue pas dans la création de ses boutiques qui réunissent une grand variété de matériaux pour renforcer leur image de marque.

La intensidad de los patrones, los tejidos y las ilustraciones de la firma barcelonesa no disminuye en el diseño de sus tiendas, que aglutinan una gran variedad de materiales para reforzar su imagen de marca.

L'intensità che caratterizza i modelli, i tessuti e le illustrazioni della marca barcellonese è comune anche al design dei suoi negozi che condensano una grande varietà di materiali per rafforzare la sua immagine di marca.

Furniture
Das Mobiliar
Le mobilier
El mobiliario
I mobili

Furniture and objects to decorate are an important help for the displaying of products. There are three different versions: stylistically, as an object of art that sets scenes; functionally, as physical support in the layout of goods, and commercially through its personalization with the trademark or the institution to whom is serving. Nowadays, using less static versions of furniture is very popular; related to space, specific areas of display can be created with the dynamic and articulated layout of fixed or mobile pieces.

Using furniture, in any of its versions, leads to the creation of displays that will collaborate with the store window conceptualisation and layout. Some of these objects are already part of the mood, the language and the aesthetics of the displaying space: having manikins is so usual that they have already suffered their own functional, material and aesthetic evolution. A manikin is not essential, but has to be in harmony with the product or the trademark. There are other complementary elements, such as the stores' sign, decorative objects to give theatrical environments or the showing of prices, that can be presented in many different ways: from ones being very discreet to others being really flashy, specially in sales promotions and in the sales.

Möbel und Dekorationsobjekte sind die besten Hilfsmittel zum Ausstellen der Produkte. Es gibt sie in drei verschiedenen Versionen, stilistisch als Kunstwerke, die Szenen künstlerisch gestalten, funktionell als physischer Träger für die Verteilung der Ware, und kommerziell zur Personalisierung der Marke oder Institution, der sie dienen. Es ist eine zeitgenössische Tendenz, nicht statisch wirkende Versionen zu verwenden, so dass durch eine dynamische und gegliederte Anordnung von festen oder beweglichen Teilen spezifische Ausstellungsbereiche geschaffen werden.

Die Benutzung von Möbeln, egal in welcher Version, führt zur Schaffung einer Dekoration, die bei der Inszenierung und Ausstattung eines Schaufensters mitwirken. Einige Objekte gehören zum Charakter, zur Ausdrucksweise und zur Ästhetik eines Schaufensters. So zum Beispiel die Schaufensterpuppen, die fast immer anzutreffen sind und die bereits eine funktionelle, materielle und ästhetische Evolution durchgemacht haben. Schaufensterpuppen sind nicht unentbehrlich, ihr Einsatz sollte mit dem Konzept übereinstimmen, das für die Marke oder das Produkt definiert wurde. Hinzu kommen ergänzende Elemente wie das Schild des Geschäftes, die Dekorationselemente, die eine theatrale Atmosphäre unterstreichen oder die Preisschilder, die es in vielen Ausführungen gibt, von ganz diskret bis zu auffallend und grell, vor allem für Verkaufskampagnen und Ausverkauf.

La présence de mobilier et objets de décoration constitue une des plus grandes aides dans l'exposition de produits. Ils se présentent dans trois versions différentes : du point de vue du style comme l'objet d'art qui réalise une mise en scène ; fonctionnelle, comme support physique dans la distribution de marchandises, et commercialement, par sa personnalisation avec la marque ou l'institution à laquelle il sert. Actuellement l'emploi de versions peu statiques de mobilier est chaque fois plus populaire ; on peut créer spatialement des secteurs spécifiques d'exposition par la disposition dynamique et articulée de pièces fixes ou mobiles.

L'utilisation du mobilier, quelle qu'elle soit sa version, conduit à créer des décors destinées à collaborer avec la création et l'ambiance de la vitrine. Quelques objets font déjà partie du caractère, du langage et de l'esthétique propres de l'espace présenté : la présence des mannequins est si habituelle qu'ils ont déjà souffert leur propre évolution fonctionnelle, matérielle et esthétique. La présence du mannequin n'est pas indispensable, mais elle doit s'harmoniser avec le concept défini para la marque ou le produit. D'autres éléments complémentaires, comme l'enseigne du magasin, les objets décoratifs pour renforcer des atmosphères théâtrales ou la affichage des prix acquièrent une grande variété de répertoires formels : des plus discrets aux plus voyants, surtout en saisons de promotions ou soldes.

La presencia de mobiliario y objetos de decoración constituye una de las mayores ayudas en la exhibición de productos. Se presentan en tres versiones distintas: estilísticamente, como objeto de arte que ambienta escenas; funcionalmente, como soporte físico en la distribución de mercancías, y comercialmente, con su personalización con la marca o la institución a la cual sirve. En la actualidad es cada vez más popular el empleo de versiones poco estáticas de mobiliario; espacialmente pueden crearse áreas específicas de exposición mediante la disposición dinámica y articulada de piezas fijas o móviles.

La utilización del mobiliario, en cualquiera de sus versiones, lleva a la creación de unos decorados destinados a colaborar con la conceptualización y la ambientación del escaparate. Algunos objetos ya forman parte del carácter, el lenguaje y la estética propios del espacio expositor: la presencia de los maniquíes es tan habitual que ya han sufrido su propia evolución funcional, material y estética. La presencia del maniquí no es indispensable, pero sí debe armonizar con el concepto definido por la marca o el producto. Otros elementos complementarios, como el rótulo de la tienda, los objetos decorativos para potenciar ambientes teatrales o la señalética de los precios adquieren una gran variedad de repertorios formales: desde los más discretos hasta los más llamativos, sobre todo en temporadas de promociones o rebajas.

La presenza di mobili e oggetti di arredo costituisce uno dei principali strumenti di supporto per l'esposizione di prodotti. I mobili possono avere tre tipi di funzione diverse: stilistica, come oggetti d'arte che ambientano le scene; funzionale, come supporto fisico nella distribuzione delle merci, e commerciale, mediante la loro personalizzazione con il marchio dell'azienda o dell'istituzione interessata. Attualmente è sempre più comune l'uso di versioni poco statiche dei mobili; sul piano dello spazio si possono creare infatti specifiche aree espositive mediante la disposizione dinamica ed articolata di elementi fissi o mobili.

Ad ogni modo, l'utilizzo dei mobili, in qualsiasi delle loro versioni, porta alla creazione di scenari che supportano l'elaborazione concettuale e l'ambientazione della vetrina. Alcuni oggetti formano già parte del carattere, del linguaggio e l'estetica propri dello spazio espositivo: la presenza dei manichini è così abituale che questi hanno già subito la loro evoluzione funzionale, materiale ed estetica. La presenza del manichino non è indispensabile, ma va indubbiamente armonizzata con il concetto definito dalla marca o dal prodotto. Altri elementi complementari, come l'insegna del negozio, gli oggetti decorativi per potenziare ambienti teatrali o la segnaletica dei prezzi assumono una grande varietà di forme: si va da quelle più discrete a quelle più appariscenti, soprattutto nei periodi promozionali o degli sconti.

Chanel

Photography: Louis Bou Romero
Barcelona, Spain

Chanel reinvents Christmas store windows with a great abstract tree where ornaments gain all the prominence and, on another side create a theatrical scenario. They give support to some of the complements of the trademark.

Chanel interpretiert das weihnachtliche Schaufenster mit einem großen, abstrakten Baum neu. Der Baumschmuck wird zum wichtigsten Element und schafft eine theatrale Atmosphäre; außerdem dient er als Ausstellungselement für Accessoires der Firma.

Chanel réinvente les vitrines de Nöel avec un grand arbre abstrait, où les ornements sont protagonistes et non seulement ils créent une scène théâtrale mais ils servent aussi de support pour certains des compléments de la marque.

Chanel reinventa los escaparates navideños con un gran árbol abstracto, donde los ornamentos cobran todo el protagonismo y aparte de crear un escenario teatral, sirven como soporte apara algunos de los complementos de la firma.

Chanel reinventa le vetrine natalizie con un grande albero astratto, dove gli addobbi rivestono tutto il protagonismo e oltre a creare uno scenario teatrale, servono da supporto per alcuni accessori della maison francese.

Hermès

Photography: Louis Bou Romero
Barcelona, Spain

HERMÈS

Luxury and sophistication are both represented in Hermès store windows. A quilted envelope is the frame of some swings made of saddles from which hang the different products of this trademark.

Die Schaufenster von Hermès wirken sehr luxuriös und edel. Eine gepolsterte Umhüllung dient als Rahmen für einige Schaukeln aus Reitsätteln, von denen verschiedene Produkte der Firma hängen.

Luxe et sophistication sont présents à parts égales dans les vitrines d'Hermès. Une enveloppante capitonnée sert de fond pour des balançoires faîtes de selles à monter d'où on accroche les différents produits de la marque.

Lujo y sofisticación están presentes a partes iguales en los escaparates de Hermès. Una envolvente acolchada sirve de marco para unos columpios compuestos de sillas de montar donde se cuelgan los distintos productos de la firma.

Nelle vetrine di Hermès il lusso e l'eleganza sono distribuiti sempre con equità. Un involucro imbottito funge da cornice per delle originali altalene formate da selle dove vengono appesi i diversi prodotti dell'azienda.

Asprey

Photography: Louis Bou Romero
London, United Kingdom

Drama, overflowing imagination and not much furniture create a particular universe with influences from 1950's and also from classic mansions of the victorian era.

Die Theatralik, die ungeheure Vorstellungskraft und einige wenige Möbelstücke lassen ein ungewöhnliches Universum entstehen, das auf die Ästhetik der Fünfzigerjahre und die klassischen Villen im viktorianischen Stil anspielt.

La théâtralité, l'imagination débordante, et quelques pièces de mobilier donnent lieu à un univers particulier, avec des réminiscences esthétiques des années 1950 et aux demeures classiques de style victorien.

La teatralidad, la imaginación desbordada y unas pocas piezas de mobiliario dan lugar a un universo particular, con reminiscencias estéticas de los años cincuenta y de las mansiones clásicas de estilo victoriano.

La teatralità, la straripante immaginazione, e pochi articoli di arredo danno vita a un universo particolare, con reminiscenze estetiche degli anni 50' che riecheggiano le mansioni classiche di stile vittoriano.

Calvin Klein

Photography: Vincent Knapp
New York, USA

sortie de
secours

Calvin Klein's risky bet in several of their more important stores consists in setting out manikins in peculiar positions: some of them as if they were to plunge into the void, others in erotic poses, some stiffed ...

Die Firma Calvin Klein setzt in einigen ihrer wichtigsten Shops auf eine riskante Linie. Schaufensterpuppen werden in eigenartigen Positionen ausgestellt, einige, als ob sie sich ins Leere stürzen würden, andere in erotischen Posen, andere wieder gestreckt ...

La parie osé de Calvin Klein dans certaines de ses boutiques les plus significatives consiste en la disposition de mannequins dans des attitudes singulières : les uns se jettent dans le vide, d'autres dans des poses érotiques, certains allongés...

La arriesgada apuesta de Calvin Klein en algunas de sus tiendas más significativas consiste en la disposición de maniquíes en posiciones singulares: unos en actitud de arrojarse al vacío, otros en poses eróticas, algunos tumbados...

L'audace proposta di Calvin Klein in alcuni dei suoi store più emblematici consiste nella peculiare disposizione dei manichini: alcuni ancora sembrano quasi sul punto di gettarsi nel vuoto, altri in atteggiamenti e pose erotiche, altri stirati...

Energie

Photography: Yael Pincus
Milan, Italy

In most cases, the store window is treated as an scenic space, as if it was a set, so it is usual that they take known pieces of design as the Charles and Ray Eames chair used in this store.

Das Schaufenster wird meist als Bühne behandelt, so als ob es sich um ein Bühnenbild handle. Oft werden bekannte Designobjekte verwendet, so z. B. der Stuhl von Charles und Ray Eames, der in diesem Geschäft zu sehen ist.

La vitrine est traité dans la plupart des cas comme un espace scénique, comme s'il s'agissait d'un décors, c'est pourquoi il est fréquent qu'on ait recours à des pièces exclusives, comme la chaise de Charles et Ray Eames utilisée dans ce boutique.

El escaparate se trata en la mayoría de los casos como un espacio escénico, como si de un decorado se tratase, por lo que es habitual que se recurra a reconocidas piezas de diseño, como la silla de Charles y Ray Eames utilizada en esta tienda.

Nella maggior parte dei casi, la vetrina viene concepita come uno spazio scenico, come se si trattasse di una scenografia, per cui è comune far ricorso a riconosciuti elementi di design come la sedia di Charles e Ray Eames utilizzata in questo negozio.

Fendi

Photography: Matteo Piazza   Design: Lazzarini & Pickering Architects
Milan, Italy

Nowadays, the stores present a lot of common features with the art galleries because the product is displayed as if it really was a piece of art. This trend is obvious when designing exclusive furniture.

Heutzutage haben Geschäfte vieles mit Kunstgalerien gemeinsam, da die Produkte oft wie wahre Kunstwerke ausgestellt werden. Dieser Trend zeigt sich auch im Design exklusiver Möbel.

Aujourd'hui, les boutiques présentent beaucoup d'aspects communs avec les galeries d'art puisque le produit est exposé comme une véritable oeuvre d'art. Cette tendance est évidente dans la création de meubles exclusifs.

Hoy en día, las tiendas presentan muchos aspectos comunes con las galerías de arte, ya que el producto se expone como si fuera una verdadera obra artística. Esta tendencia se hace evidente en el diseño de muebles exclusivos.

Oggigiorno, i negozi presentano molti aspetti in comune con le gallerie d'arte visto che il prodotto si espone come se fosse una vera e propria opera d'arte. Questa tendenza si evidenzia nel disegno di mobili esclusivi.